First edition
By Lea Coquille Chambel

Don't store it, hide it

YOU ARE THE ONLY ONE WHO KNOWS WHAT YOU ARE GOING THROUGH, WHAT YOU THINK AND WHO YOU ARE

In 2021, as a result of the various lockdowns, the possibility of physical contact with people has been reduced and loneliness has become widespread.
Mental health is more and more fragile for some people and this book will help you to free yourself, to say out loud what you quietly think.

Speak up and free your mind.

In a world where everything you do is scrutinized, free yourself from those sentences you dare to not say to anyone.

This journal offers you the possibility to share your thoughts without any criticism.

ENJOY ANSWERING A SERIES OF QUESTIONS WITHOUT WORRYING ABOUT WHAT OTHERS MIGHT THINK.

DON'T STORE IT, HIDE IT

BE HONEST

You and only you have access to this journal, be honest, accept yourself.

Looking a fool never killed anyone.

Gain confidence and get to know yourself in a fun way.

The purpose of this book is for you to discover yourself, to express yourself.

DO NOT SHARE ANY PAGE OF THIS BOOK AND CONFESS.

DON'T STORE IT, HIDE IT

IF I HAD TO GO BACK IN TIME IT WOULD BE AT THE TIME :

MY BIGGEST PLEASURE :

AND CRUSH :

THE THING I LIKE THE MOST :

THE THING I LIKE THE LEAST :

IF I COULD START A CHARITY, IT WOULD BE :

STRANGERS THINK MY AGE IS :

THE CHORE I HATE :

I AM DRAWING WHAT COMES TO MY MIND

MY BIGGEST SHAME :

THE MOMENT I WOULD LIKE TO RELIVE :

+ OR - TRUE

I make friends easily	- -	-	o	+	++
I don't like clutter	- -	-	o	+	++
I easily trust	- -	-	o	+	++
I often feel sad	- -	-	o	+	++
I keep my promises	- -	-	o	+	++
I hate routine	- -	-	o	+	++
I act without thinking	- -	-	o	+	++
I panic quickly	- -	-	o	+	++
I often feel alone	- -	-	o	+	++
I feel comfortable in a crowd	- -	-	o	+	++
I get easily irritated	- -	-	o	+	++
I easily get down to work	- -	-	o	+	++
I like myself	- -	-	o	+	++
I like being under pressure	- -	-	o	+	++
I am unsympathetic	- -	-	o	+	++

+ OR - TRUE

I often lie	- -	-	o	+	++
I like to be the center of the world	- -	-	o	+	++
I have a lot of fun	- -	-	o	+	++
I am easily scared	- -	-	o	+	++
I dream a lot	- -	-	o	+	++
I spend a lot of time on Netflix	- -	-	o	+	++
I prefer to be alone	- -	-	o	+	++
I go against the rules	- -	-	o	+	++
I get stressed out quickly	- -	-	o	+	++
I am messy	- -	-	o	+	++
I feel good about myself	- -	-	o	+	++
I am hungry	- -	-	o	+	++
I hold grudges	- -	-	o	+	++
I prefer sweet to salty	- -	-	o	+	++
I have a lot of imagination	- -	-	o	+	++

THE PERSON I ADMIRE THE MOST :

....

....

....

I WAS PROUD OF MYSELF WHEN I :

....

....

....

MY OLDEST MEMORY :

....

....

....

IF MY FRIENDS HAD TO DESCRIBE ME IN 3 WORDS, THEY WOULD SAY :

1 ....

2 ....

3 ....

Is it easy for me to say no ? :

The extracurricular activity of my dreams :

An anecdote about me :

In the morning I get up at :

GOING TO A PARTY WHERE I DON'T KNOW ANYONE, POSSIBLE ? :

A HOLIDAY ROMANCE ? :

WHAT TERRIFIES ME :

I AM JEALOUS OF :

A typical Sunday in my childhood :

A typical Sunday now :

MY DEFINITION OF LOVE :

....

....

....

....

THE PLACE WHERE I FEEL MOST COMFORTABLE :

....

....

....

IF I COULD AVOID DOING SOMETHING FOR THE REST OF MY LIFE :

....

....

....

I WISH MY NAME WAS :

....

....

....

OVER TIME, I HAVE LEARNED THAT :

BUT ALSO THAT :

I SECRETLY HATE :

THE THING THAT COMFORTS ME THE MOST :

MY PARENTS IN 3 WORDS :

1 ....

2 ....

3 ....

MY DREAM HOUSE :

....

....

....

....

....

THE RISKS I DARE NOT TAKE :

....

....

....

....

....

....

The person who / that

Is the funniest :

Is the most talkative :

Is always late :

Made me cry the most :

Dresses best :

Likes money the most :

Is alway cold :

Eats the most unhealthy :

Is the dumbest :

Could be on survivor :

Hurt me the most :

Is the most important :

I can't forget :

Could be on a reality show :

I regret having met :

Can live a week without showering :

Lies the most :

Is the proudest of me :

The person who / that

Can create the most problems :

Does illegal things :

Likes soccer the most :

Can become famous :

Is the most annoying :

Can end up in jail :

Is the least funny :

Will get married first :

Would be there if I couldn't move anymore :

Would give me the best gift :

And the worst one :

Is often in my dreams :

Is my secret crush :

Spends too much time on their phone :

Speaks French the best :

Could sing in the subway :

Could rob someone :

Could cheat on someone :

THE BEST THING I HAVE EVER DONE :

AND THE WORST :

MY FAVORITE DISNEY HERO :

I would like to learn :

....

....

....

....

....

....

If my house burns, I would take with me :

....

....

....

The power of my dreams :

....

....

....

My level of education :

....

....

....

MY BEST MOMENT OF THE DAY :

IF I COULD THANK SOMEONE IT WOULD BE :

I WOULD SAY TO THEM :

1+1+1

3 THINGS I ALWAYS CARRY WITH ME :

   1

   2

   3

3 OF MY STRENGTHS :

   1

   2

   3

3 OF MY WEAKNESSES :

   1

   2

   3

3 MISTAKES I MADE :

   1

   2

   3

1 + 1 + 1

3 things I need now :

1
2
3

The first 3 songs on shuffle :

1
2
3

3 things that make me laugh :

1
2
3

3 things I find ridiculous :

1
2
3

1+1+1

3 THINGS THAT ANNOY ME :

1 ....

2 ....

3 ....

3 THINGS I DO WHEN I GET UP :

1 ....

2 ....

3 ....

3 THINGS I DO WHEN I GO TO BED :

1 ....

2 ....

3 ....

3 MOST IMPORTANT THINGS :

1 ....

2 ....

3 ....

My favorite smell :

If I didn't need to sleep anymore, instead I would :

My biggest financial expense :

1 flaw I can't stand in my friends :

IF I COULD GO BACK 1 YEAR I WOULD CHANGE

A true friend for me is :

The bias I had about each of my friends :

These days, before I go to sleep, I think about

My worst date :

If I had to eat only 1 thing for 1 month :

My most destructive relationship :

My parent's profession :

Any contact with my exes ? :

The part of the body that attracts me the most :

I have been in love before ? :

THE CELEBRITY WHO LOOKS LIKE ME THE MOST :

MY LAST TRIP :

3 PHYSICAL QUALITIES IN ME :

    1

    2

    3

OFTEN LATE ? :

My dream evening :

The craziest thing I've ever done :

A religion :

If I could change one thing in the world :

During summer break, I :

My first word :

When the weather is good, I :

The historical fact that most affected me :

What I would have liked to change in my childhood :

My favorite food as a child :

The first film I saw in a cinema :

THE CELEBRITY WHO / THAT

Taught me things :

Grew up with me :

Could be my bff (woman) :

Could be my bff (man) :

Was my crush when I was younger :

Is my crush today :

Who will remain my crush for life :

Gives me the most confidence :

Gives me the least confidence :

Inspires me the most :

Irritates me the most :

Makes me laugh the most :

I would like to meet :

I have seen :

I like the most :

I am ashamed of loving :

Deceived me :

I find hot :

MY PERFECT DAY :

....

....

....

....

....

I STILL LIKE :

....

....

....

....

THE RELATIONSHIP I WOULD LIKE TO IMPROVE :

....

....

....

....

I CAN DIE FOR :

THE WORST MESSAGE I HAVE EVER SENT :

MY FAVORITE FAMILY TRADITION :

MY FAVORITE BIRTHDAY :

THE PERSON I HATE THE MOST :

My best moment of the year

When I was younger, I used to spend my pocket money on :

....

....

....

....

....

....

My last relationship lasted :

....

....

....

....

My opinion on love at first sight :

....

....

....

....

A word for my ex

My to do list (before I die)

- [ ] ....
- [ ] ....
- [ ] ....
- [ ] ....
- [ ] ....
- [ ] ....
- [ ] ....
- [ ] ....
- [ ] ....
- [ ] ....
- [ ] ....
- [ ] ....
- [ ] ....
- [ ] ....
- [ ] ....
- [ ] ....
- [ ] ....
- [ ] ....
- [ ] ....
- [ ] ....

Dear me,

My wallpaper :

I could be famous because :

My favorite sport :

My favorite influencers :

How I would react to :

A zombie apocalypse :

No social media for a week :

Waking up on a desert island :

Getting married tomorrow :

Getting 1M $:

An invitation to THE OSCARS :

MY FAVORITE APP :

....

....

....

MY BOYFRIEND / GIRLFRIEND TYPE :

....

....

....

....

I AM NO LONGER WITH MY EX BECAUSE :

....

....

....

....

....

....

The best advice I have ever gotten :

The thing I would like to accomplish :

My relationship to money :

MY FAVORITE JOKE :

HOW I MET MY BEST FRIEND :

IF I WERE TO CREATE 3 RULES THAT OTHERS MUST RESPECT TOWARDS ME :

1 ....

2 ....

3 ....

IF I COULD CHANGE SOMETHING ABOUT MY BODY :

....

....

....

....

AND MY PERSONALITY :

....

....

....

....

....

....

....

MY MOST EMBARRASSING MOMENTS

A drawing of the thing I like the most

A DRAWING OF THE THING I LIKE THE LEAST

Rating myself :

Self-confidence : 10% 20% 30% 40% 50% 60% 70% 80% 90% 100%

Determination : 10% 20% 30% 40% 50% 60% 70% 80% 90% 100%

Patience : 10% 20% 30% 40% 50% 60% 70% 80% 90% 100%

My respect : 10% 20% 30% 40% 50% 60% 70% 80% 90% 100%

Honesty : 10% 20% 30% 40% 50% 60% 70% 80% 90% 100%

Humor : 10% 20% 30% 40% 50% 60% 70% 80% 90% 100%

Intelligence : 10% 20% 30% 40% 50% 60% 70% 80% 90% 100%

Tolerance : 10% 20% 30% 40% 50% 60% 70% 80% 90% 100%

Solidarity : 10% 20% 30% 40% 50% 60% 70% 80% 90% 100%

Sociability : 10% 20% 30% 40% 50% 60% 70% 80% 90% 100%

Creativity : 10% 20% 30% 40% 50% 60% 70% 80% 90% 100%

Style : 10% 20% 30% 40% 50% 60% 70% 80% 90% 100%

Health : 10% 20% 30% 40% 50% 60% 70% 80% 90% 100%

Generosity : 10% 20% 30% 40% 50% 60% 70% 80% 90% 100%

Concentration : 10% 20% 30% 40% 50% 60% 70% 80% 90% 100%

Talent : 10% 20% 30% 40% 50% 60% 70% 80% 90% 100%

Physique : 10% 20% 30% 40% 50% 60% 70% 80% 90% 100%

An unspeakable secret

THE AMOUNT I NEED IN MY ACCOUNT :

SO I CAN BUY :

THE WORST MESSAGE I'VE EVER RECEIVED :

The last time I had the giggles :

My favorite activity :

The thing I can't admit to myself :

I have imaginary friends ? :

The only person who knows my secrets :

My dream friend :

This or that

Camping	Or	Hotel
Hot	Or	Cold
Tv	Or	YouTube
Tv show	Or	Movie
Summer	Or	Winter
Kendall	Or	Kylie
Day	Or	Night
Dad	Or	Mom
Coca Cola	Or	Ice tea
Instagram	Or	Tiktok

This or that

Piercing	Or	Tattoo
Party	Or	Sleeping
Audi	Or	Mercedes
Los Angeles	Or	Dubaï
Nike	Or	Adidas
Man	Or	Woman
Intelligence	Or	Beauty
Time	Or	Money
Realistic	Or	Idealist
Rich	Or	Famous

THE TYPE OF CONTENT I WOULD LIKE TO DO ON SOCIAL MEDIA :

....

....

....

....

A TRAVEL SWEETHEART :

....

....

....

....

LINE OF A SONG THAT STUCK WITH ME :

....

....

....

....

....

My typical day on vacation

Last :

Sent message :

Received message :

Movie that I watched :

I cried :

Music I listened to :

Google search :

Received call :

Took my shower :

Laughed :

Was in love :

Was angry :

YouTube video :

Outfit :

Liked TikTok :

Drink :

Meal :

Book :

Am I rather ?

Fast	-	Slow
Leader	-	Follower
Serious	-	Carefree
Extrovert	-	Introvert
Stable	-	Unstable
Egocentric	-	Altruist
Reasoning	-	Action
Tolerance	-	Criticism
Happy	-	Sad

Destination for a week-end in Europe :

I like to be comforted by :

My qualities :

TELL AN ANECDOTE ABOUT EACH OF YOUR INSTAGRAM PHOTOS :

TELL AN ANECDOTE ABOUT EACH OF YOUR INSTAGRAM PHOTOS :

IF I COULD HAVE A WILD PET, IT WOULD BE :

MY FLAWS :

I WANT TO HAVE CHILDREN :

THE MESSAGE I DARE NOT SEND :

I LOOK MOST LIKE :

THE TREND I LIKED BEST :

What I think about Valentine's Day :

My most romantic act :

In love I look for :

My favorite things :

Location in the world :

Movie :

Tv show :

Meal :

Music :

Day of the week :

Animal :

Piece of clothing :

App :

Social media platform :

Brand :

Drink :

Season :

Artist :

Sportsman :

YouTuber :

School subject :

A romantic evening for me :

The most beautiful place I have visited :

Worst advice I have ever gotten :

From :

Dear me in 5 years,

IF I WASN'T EMBARRASSED OF ANYTHING, I WOULD :

MY WORST TRAVEL MEMORY :

MY FAVORITE VIDEO GAME :

The song that

Makes me laugh :

Gives me energy :

Makes me feel nostalgic :

Reminds me of my childhood :

That I love but hate the artist :

I am ashamed to love :

Where I love the lyrics :

That I put on in the morning :

That makes me think about holidays :

That makes me cry :

That I listen alone :

I love to sing :

I hate :

Matches my mood at the moment :

Reminds me of the person I love :

That I wish I had written :

Reminds me of my ex :

My song of the moment :

An unspeakable secret

MY MOST FAMOUS CONTACT :

WHAT I THINK OF INSTAGRAM :

MY DREAM TRIP :

LIVING WITHOUT SPORT OR SOCIAL MEDIA :

WHAT I THINK OF TIKTOK :

THE KIND OF VIDEO I WOULDN'T DARE TO MAKE ON TIKTOK :

I CAN LEAVE EVERYTHING FOR :

The most beautiful thing I've ever seen :

Right now I would like to receive a call from :

The last person I blocked :

I am currently in a mood :

What if I left / gave up on ? :

A person :

A habit :

An expression :

A song :

An influencer :

An outfit :

A meal :

A drink :

An addiction :

A color :

A Tv show :

An activity :

A fast-food :

A brand :

A family member :

A dream :

A memory :

Do I accept or not ?

Deception :

Lies :

Violence :

Disrespect :

Hypocrisy :

Impatience :

Selfishness :

Arrogance :

Criticism :

Rudeness :

Lack of manners :

Instability :

Secrecy :

Lack of style :

Lack of humour :

Harassment :

Immaturity :

The biggest secret I keep inside
(write on the page, cut out the page, destroy the page)

The biggest secret I keep inside
(write on the page, cut out the page, destroy the page)

92

I draw what hurt me the most
(draw on the page, cut out the page, destroy the page)

I DRAW WHAT HURT ME THE MOST
(DRAW ON THE PAGE, CUT OUT THE PAGE, DESTROY THE PAGE)

I express myself
(write on the page, cut out the page, destroy the page)

I EXPRESS MYSELF
(WRITE ON THE PAGE, CUT OUT THE PAGE, DESTROY THE PAGE)

Do you feel like you have said it all ?
Are you still lying to yourself ?

☐ Yes   ☐ No

Yes -> destroy this book

No -> read the questions again, correct yourself, let go

TO START AGAIN WITHOUT LIMITATION :)

PS : BELIEVE IN YOURSELF

DON'T STORE IT, HIDE IT

Printed in Great Britain
by Amazon